THE NIGHTMARE BEFORE CHRISTMAS

TAROT DECK
AND GUIDEBOOK

WRITTEN BY
Minerva Siegel

ILLUSTRATED BY
Abigail Larson

TITAN BOOKS
LONDON

CONTENTS

04
Introduction

06
Understanding Your Tarot Deck

11
The Major Arcana

The Fool 12

I The Magician 14

II The High Priestess 16

III The Empress 18

IV The Emperor 20

V The Hierophant 22

VI The Lovers 24

VII The Chariot 26

VIII Strength 28

IX The Hermit 30

X The Wheel of Fortune 32

XI Justice 34

XII The Hanged Man 36

XIII Death 38

XIV Temperance 40
XV The Devil 42
XVI The Tower 44
XVII The Star 46
XVIII The Moon 48
XIX The Sun 50
XX Judgment 52
XXI The World 54

57
The Minor Arcana
Suit of Candles 58
Suit of Presents 72
Suit of Needles 86
Suit of Potions 100

115
Tarot Readings
Caring for Your Deck 117
Preparing to Read Tarot 118
The Spreads 120

INTRODUCTION

Welcome to *The Nightmare Before Christmas Tarot Deck and Guidebook*! What's this, you ask? Why, a deck of tarot cards featuring the strange and mischievous characters of *The Nightmare Before Christmas*, of course. Jack, Sally, their friends, their neighbors, even that no-account Oogie Boogie, are here to help you explore your past, present, and future in the classic tradition of tarot. Whether you are a newcomer to tarot or an experienced reader, this deck is a real scream. Just try not to pull the Clown with the Tear-Away Face ... his card is definitely the stuff of nightmares.

While many people think of tarot reading as a mystical divinatory art mainly used to predict the future, it can actually be a powerful tool for personal growth and self-reflection. Tarot reading can offer deep insight into all kinds of situations in your life. It can help uncover your true feelings, provide clarity for making decisions, and show you how to get where you want to go. While some people do use tarot to reveal a possible future, it's important to remember nothing is set in stone. Tarot is best at giving situational warnings and advice that can help you make more mindful choices.

The Nightmare Before Christmas tarot deck is filled with familiar faces, themes, and iconic moments from the film, thoughtfully chosen to illustrate the archetypal meanings of the original cards. The Guidebook explains both the upright and reversed versions of each card. The final chapter includes several spreads for conducting easy readings.

Now, ready for a visit to Halloween Town? Let's go!

UNDERSTANDING YOUR TAROT DECK

Learning to read tarot can seem intimidating at first, but it's really quite easy when you get the hang of it. There are 78 tarot cards in a deck, and each one has a different meaning depending on whether it's drawn upright or reversed. The first 22 cards are called the Major Arcana. They represent important themes and major life lessons with lasting impact. Numbered zero through XXI, they chronologically tell the story of the Fool (the first card in the Major Arcana), a figure who takes an exciting and sometimes harrowing journey that ultimately leads to enlightenment and fulfillment. In *The Nightmare Before Christmas* tarot deck, the journey of the Major Arcana is representative of the adventures of the Pumpkin King himself, Jack Skellington, who takes the Fool's traditional place as card number zero.

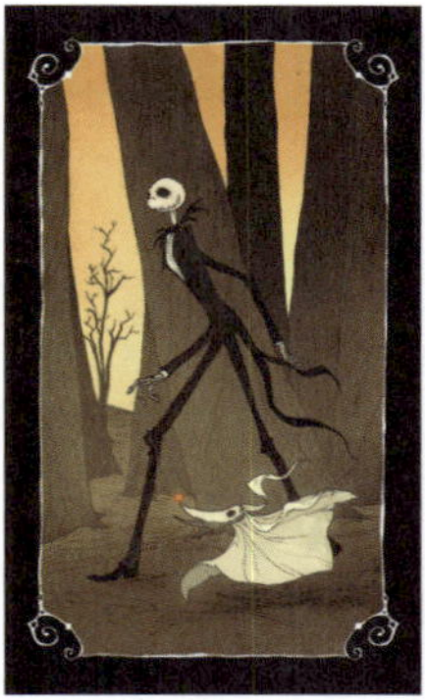
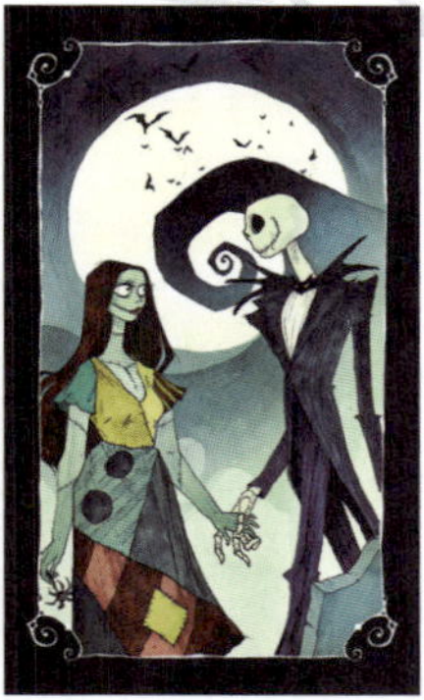
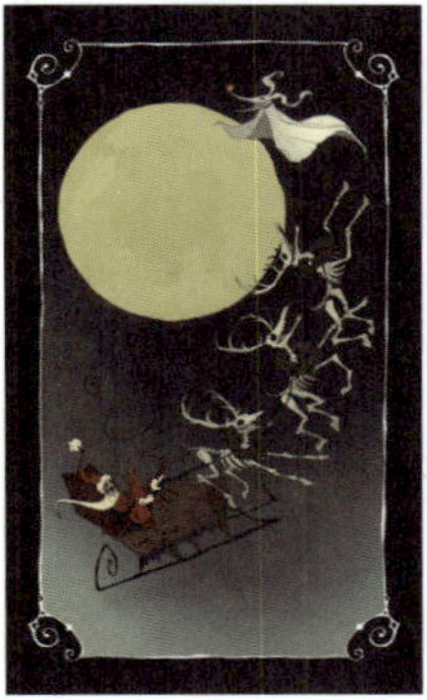
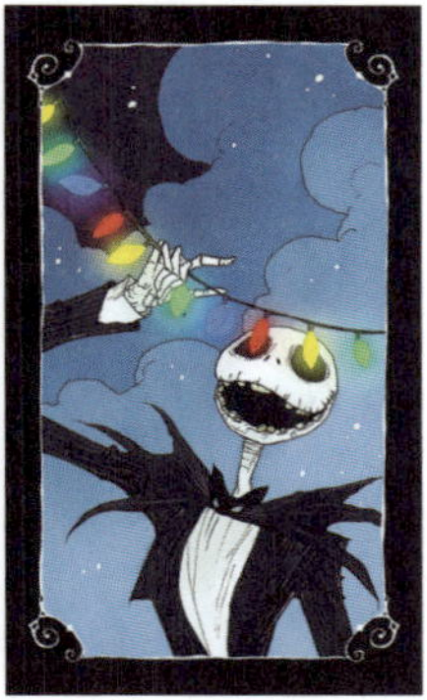

The rest of the tarot cards in the deck are called Minor Arcana. Representing everyday situations and themes with short-term effects, the 56 Minor Arcana cards are sorted into four suits. In *The Nightmare Before Christmas* tarot deck, the four suits are Potions, Candles, Needles, and Presents, which are representative of the traditional tarot suits of Cups, Wands, Swords, and Pentacles, respectively.

The suit of Potions deals with emotions, personal connections with family or friends, and relationships. It corresponds to the element of water.

The suit of Candles is associated with ideas, creativity, inspiration, and ambition. It corresponds to the element of fire.

The suit of Needles refers to the mind, intellect, power, judgment, and personal beliefs. It corresponds to the element of air.

The suit of Presents is associated with aspects of the material world and our relationship to it, such as finances, careers, property, home, and the ego. It corresponds to the element of earth.

Each of these suits contains four court cards: the Page, Knight, Queen, and King. They symbolize personality types, behavior patterns, and sometimes, actual people in your life. The remaining cards are numbered I (Ace) to X.

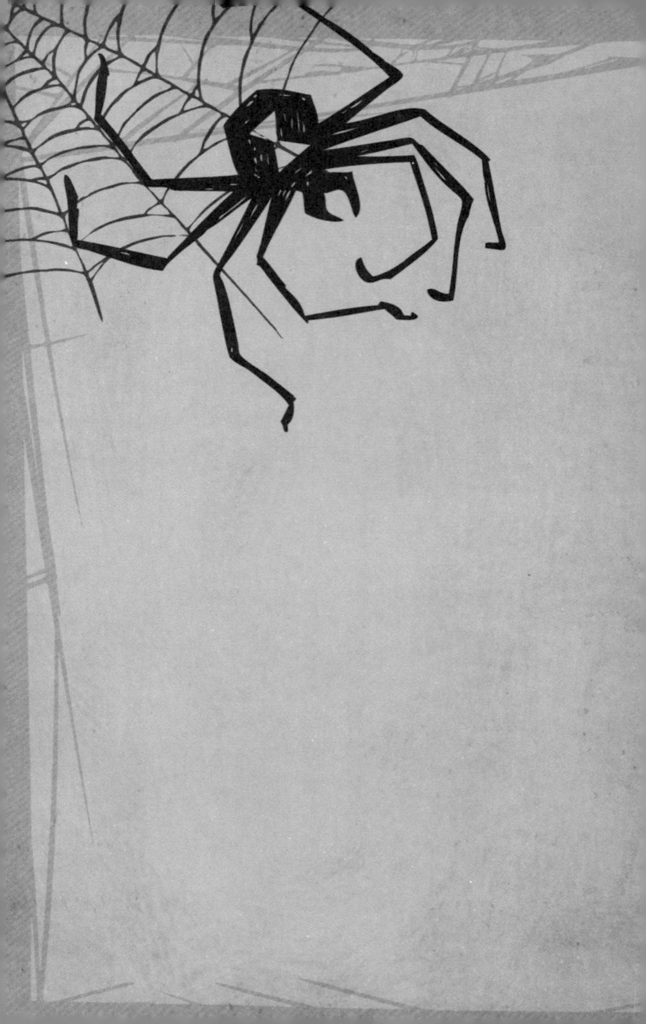

THE MAJOR ARCANA

THE FOOL

The Fool represents someone who's starting an exciting adventure. Jack Skellington, like the Fool, is enthusiastic and determined as he sets out on his ill-advised journey to take over Christmas.

Upright: Channel Jack Skellington's childlike enthusiasm as you take your first brave steps toward something new. With limitless potential, there's no telling how far you'll go.

Reversed: Jack's naivety and idealism initially blind him to the damage he causes when taking over Christmas. Learn from his mistakes: Stay excited about the future, but be sensible, and look before you leap.

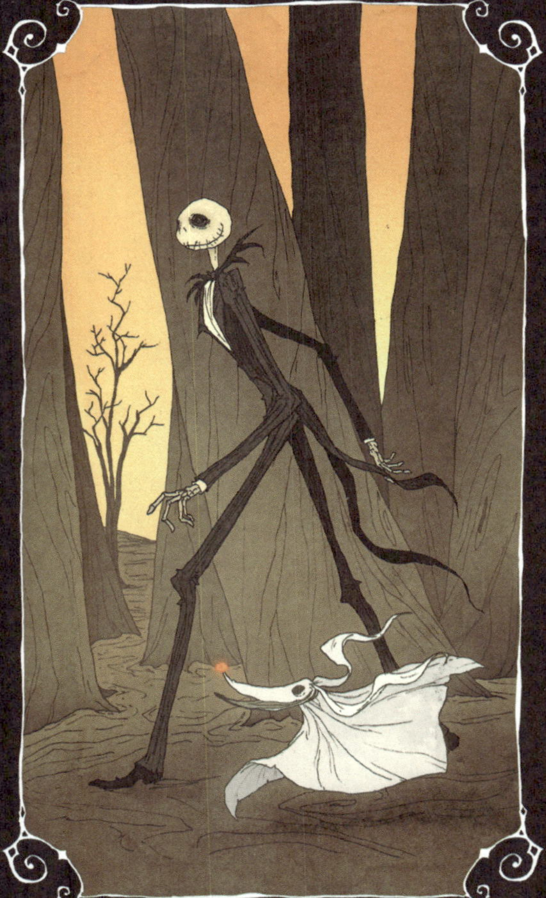

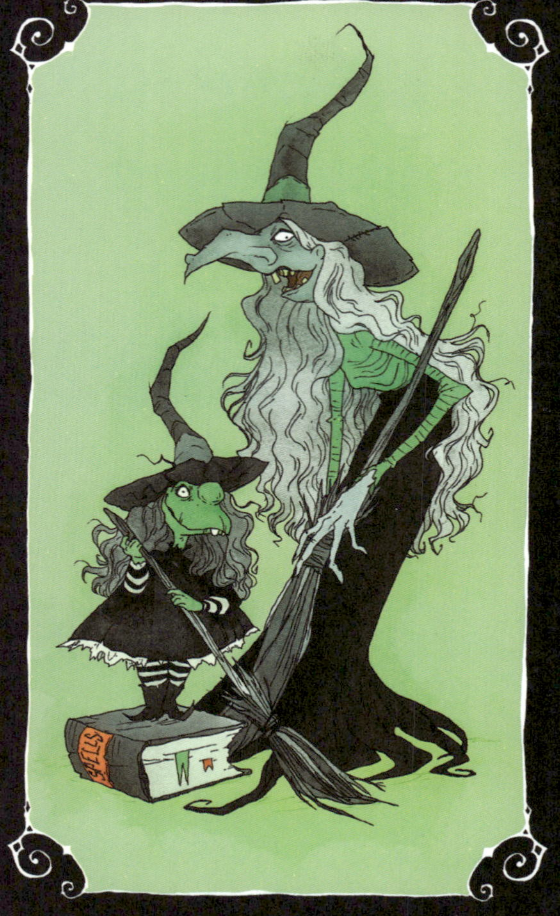
SPELLS

I · THE MAGICIAN

Like the Witches of Halloween Town, the Magician combines raw talent and ambition with focused action to manifest a magical vision.

Upright: You're bubbling over with creativity and inspiration! Now is the time to do something meaningful with it. Put action behind all of your inspired energy to make real progress. Focus, come up with a plan, and make your dreams come true.

Reversed: Have you been working hard, but not seeing the results you're expecting? Squash self-doubt with determination, and stay committed to your goals. Be careful not to let the fear of failure stop you from giving your all. Your dreams are possible! Stay dedicated to them.

II · THE HIGH PRIESTESS

Sally's perceptive and observant nature perfectly captures the energy of the High Priestess card. The High Priestess is an intuitive visionary who's tuned in to what's really going on under the surface.

Upright: Just as Sally's vision of a burning Christmas tree holds a dire warning about Jack's plans, the appearance of this card is a suggestion to beware. Situations in your own life might not be what they appear. Check in with your intuition, and trust your instincts to connect with the truth.

Reversed: The High Priestess calls for contemplation and self-reflection. Are there areas of your life that don't feel as harmonious and easy as they should? Take a step back to see hiccups for what they are. Channel Sally's brand of compassionate wisdom, and sort them out. You'll feel so much better when things are running smoothly.

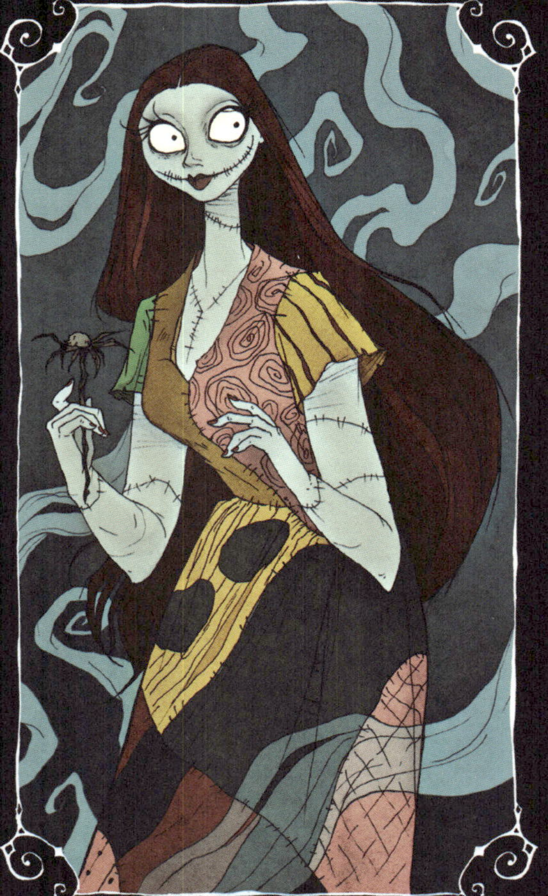

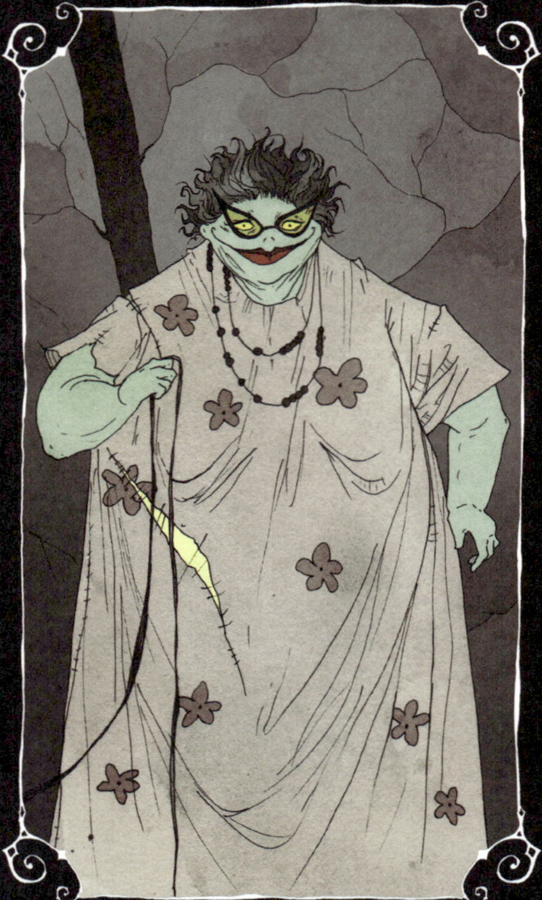

III · THE EMPRESS

The Empress is a maternal, nurturing figure who enjoys self-indulgence and life's creature comforts. Our Empress is the Corpse Mom, who is often seen leading her child on a leash.

Upright: This is a call for compassion. Being patient and kind with yourself and others will get you further than any other approach. Now's a great time to nurture and indulge your creative impulses, and staying grateful will help you keep a positive, healthy outlook.

Reversed: Are you being too hard on yourself? You may have been feeling self-critical lately, but beating yourself up about perceived failures and flaws won't help. Be patient, and give yourself room to make mistakes—they're learning opportunities.

IV · THE EMPEROR

The Emperor, like Sandy Claws, uses calm, commanding practicality to take control and save the day.

Upright: The Emperor is a levelheaded ruler and paternal figure who creates order, stability, and routine. Muster your confidence, square your shoulders, and get ready to step into a powerful role. Rather than trying to completely reinvent the wheel, rely on structure, order, and practicality to be the best leader you can be.

Reversed: Is there a major power struggle going on in your life right now? It could be you're feeling paralyzed. If someone's walking all over you, stand up for yourself. Examine and reassess your plans and daily routines, and don't be afraid to shake things up.

THE MAJOR ARCANA

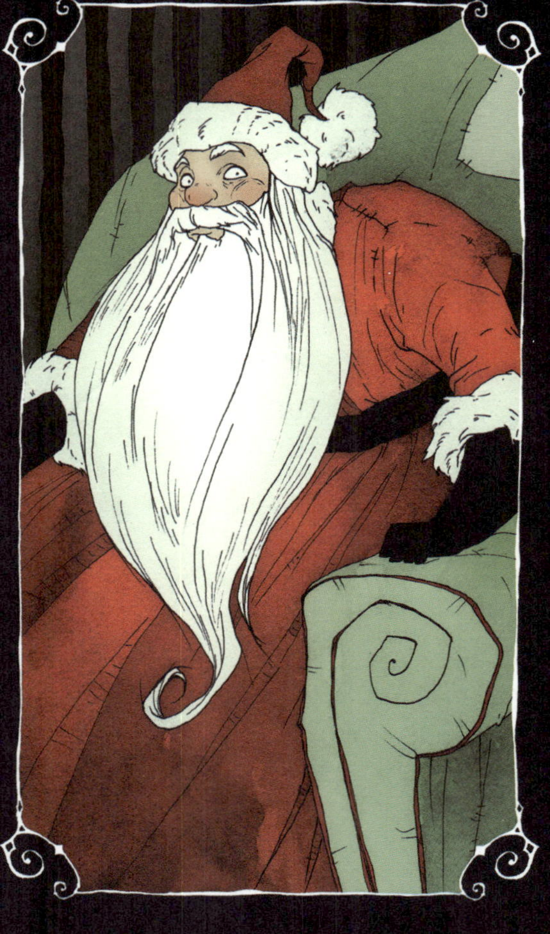

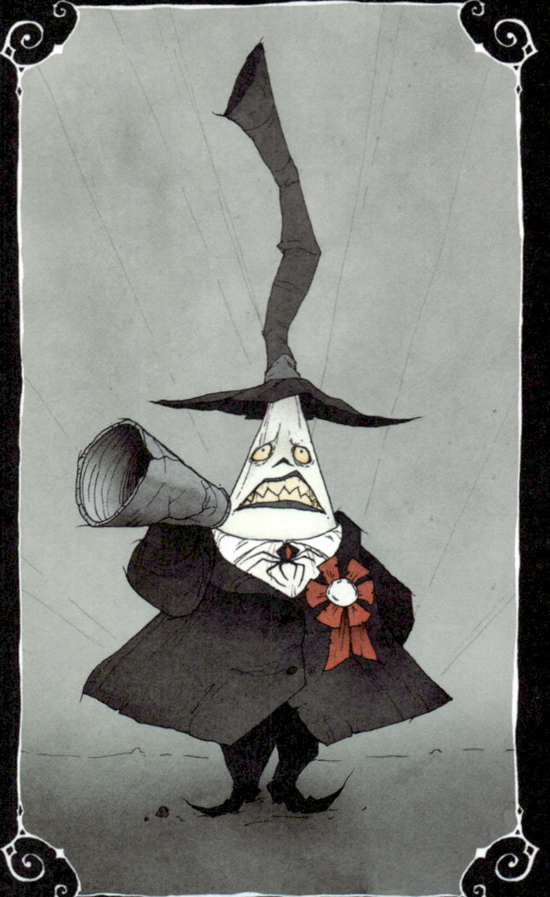

V · THE HIEROPHANT

The Hierophant is a teacher and a leader who values traditions, rules, and order just as much as the Mayor of Halloween Town.

Upright: Do you have a trusted mentor in your life? Whether they're an elected official like the Mayor, or a teacher, community leader, or spiritual counselor, look to them for guidance. Even if you don't agree with all their ideas and processes, learning from them will help you form your own opinions on how to manage your life.

Reversed: Are you feeling rebellious and dissatisfied with the status quo? It might be time to turn your back on tradition and go your own way. Trust yourself!

VI · THE LOVERS

The Lovers card represents supportive, healthy, magical connection. The Lovers fit together like Jack and Sally—they're meant to be!

Upright: You're creating meaningful friendships, connections, and relationships that will enrich your life. Build these connections on a foundation of honesty and mutual respect. There's also an element of choice in the Lovers tarot card. If you have a decision to make, don't overanalyze the situation. Decide with your heart.

Reversed: Something's off. If you're feeling at odds with someone in your life, you have a choice to make. Do you want to put the time and effort into communicating and trying to rebuild your connection, or is it best to part ways? Reflect on this relationship, and consider what you really want from it.

THE MAJOR ARCANA

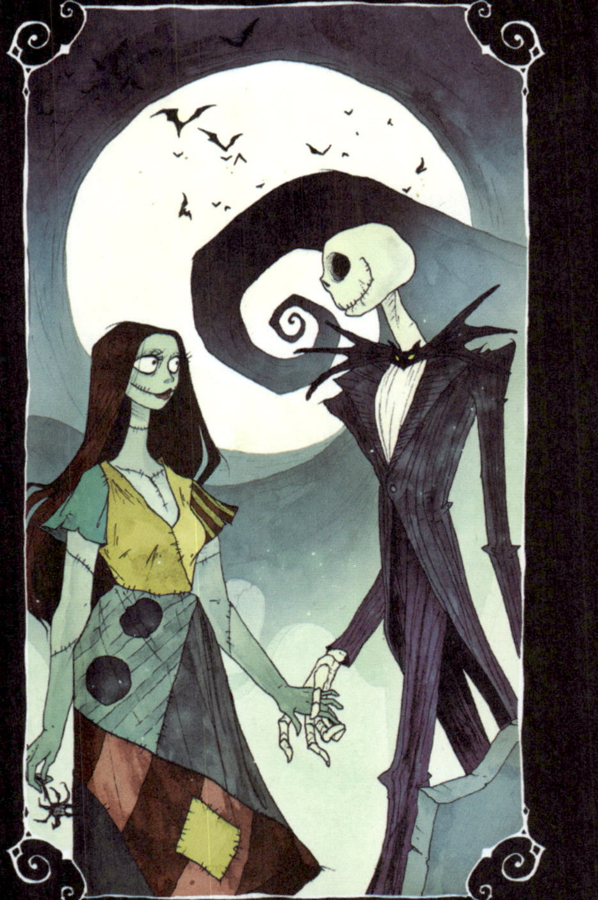

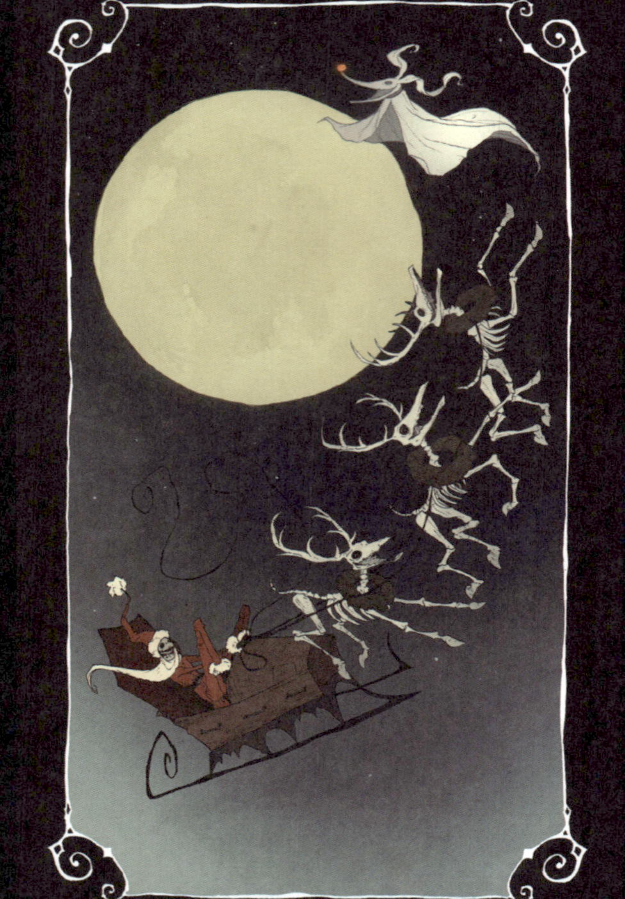

VII · THE CHARIOT

With determination, focus, and drive, Jack steers his sleigh through the night sky, delivering presents on Christmas Eve. The Chariot represents progress, forward momentum, and the harnessing of inner strength to overcome obstacles in your way.

Upright: Jack stops at nothing to make his dreams come true. This singular commitment to a goal is what the Chariot is all about! Don't get sidetracked, because there's no time for doubts. Continue forward with fierce determination, and don't let anything stand in your way.

Reversed: Are you getting bogged down in the details or discouraged by setbacks? Reconnect with your initial motivation. Remembering your goals will help you find the strength and passion you need to move forward and succeed.

VIII · STRENGTH

The Strength card represents bravery, courage, compassion, and gentle, nurturing leadership. Our incarnation of this card is the Behemoth, who is often seen using his great strength to help out around Halloween Town.

Upright: Though the Behemoth is large and imposing, he has a soft side that celebrates creatures big and small ("Bunny!"). Strength isn't just about brute force; it's about having the self-control and sense to know when to be firm and when to lead with compassion. Don't try to use force to get your way. You'll be more successful if you lead by example and stay kind.

Reversed: If you're feeling powerless, remember it's never too late to start over and live the life you envision. Regain control over your destiny by believing in yourself. You're far more powerful than you think.

THE MAJOR ARCANA

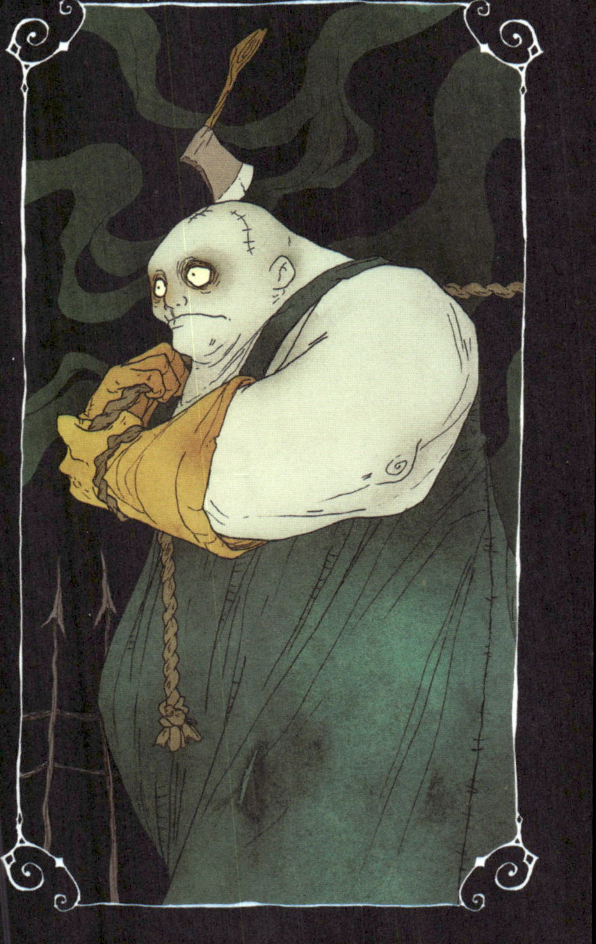

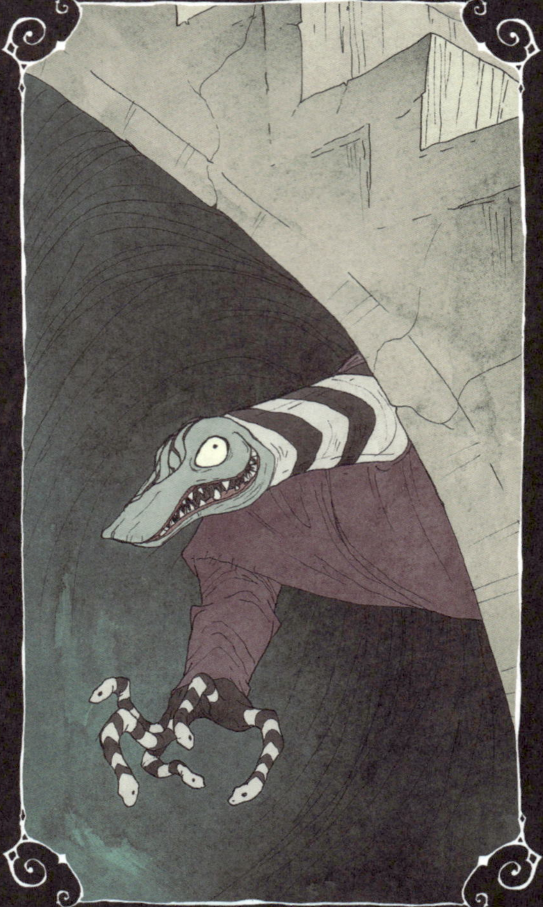

IX · THE HERMIT

The Hermit is a thoughtful, introverted figure who likes to spend his time ruminating alone—like the Creature Under the Stairs.

Upright: Now's the time to get inspired by example and withdraw for some quiet alone time. The Hermit calls for reflection, so do a bit of soul-searching. Consider your current position, goals, and dreams. Remember your past, and learn from it so you can bring those lessons with you into a successful future.

Reversed: Are you feeling overwhelmed or aimless? If you need direction, look within. You have the answers you need; to find them, make time for yourself. Getting away from the hustle and bustle of daily life will bring you much needed clarity.

X · THE WHEEL OF FORTUNE

Like Oogie Boogie's roulette wheel, the Wheel of Fortune is all about chance. This card represents major life changes and shifts in luck.

Upright: You have reached a turning point in your life—the moment when the storm clouds part, the sun comes out, and your luck begins to change. Now may be the time to make a big move. Whether you switch careers, begin a new romance, jump-start lifestyle shifts, or relocate across the country, you'll have good fortune on your side.

Reversed: Life is full of ups and downs. Everything can change in an instant, which may feel scary or even traumatic. Don't get discouraged when things seem dire, because fortune is unpredictable, and fate is at play. Stay hopeful.

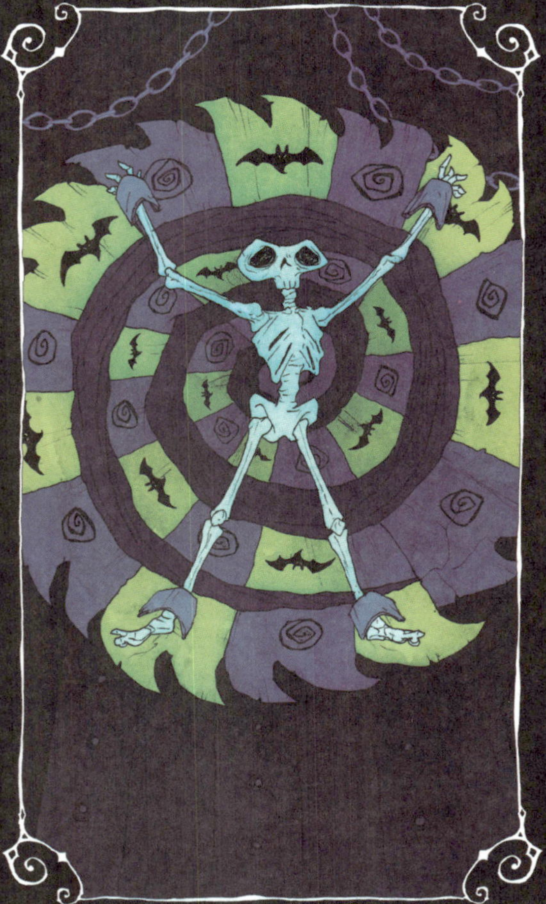

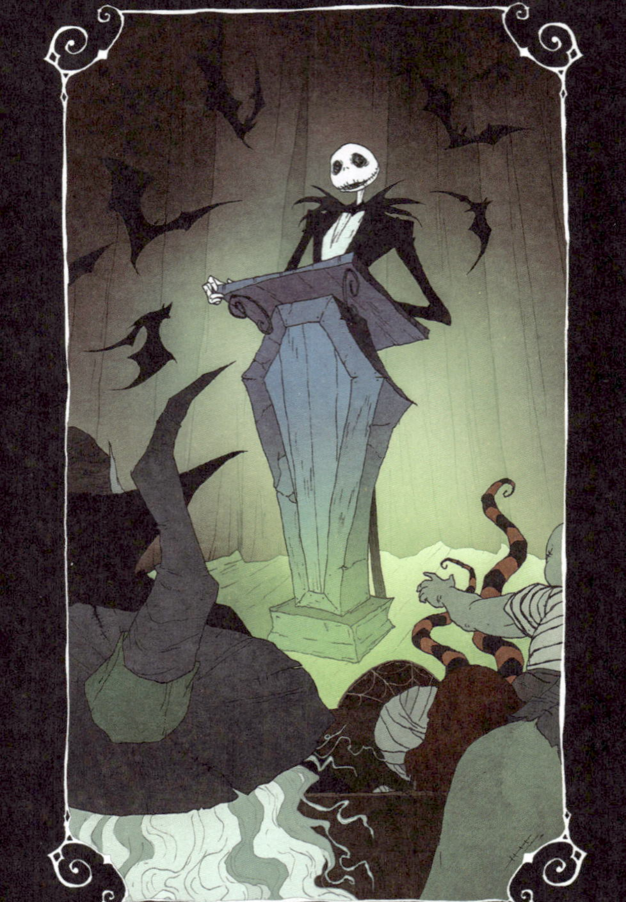

XI · JUSTICE

The residents of Halloween Town come together during town meetings to discuss important events and decisions, invoking the spirit of Justice. Justice as a tarot card is all about due course, accountability, and deciding what's fair.

Upright: You're searching for the truth, which isn't always easy. Seek out the views and opinions of others to give you a clearer perspective of what's really going on. If you're in the process of making a big decision, be sure to think about all possible outcomes, and keep future repercussions in mind.

Reversed: Are you behaving in ways that align with your conscience? Examine your personal ethics, and make sure they align with your actions. Make decisions carefully, with the law of cause and effect in mind. Whatever action you take will have a reaction, so be sensible, and be aware of consequences.

XII · THE HANGED MAN

The Hanged Man represents a great pause, unexpected delays, and the need for a shift in perspective. In this deck, the Hanged Man is represented by Sandy Claws, who's been captured in Oogie Boogie's lair.

Upright: Life is unpredictable, and your circumstances can change very quickly. It's easy to get caught up in plans, goals, and thinking about the future, but the Hanged Man reminds you it's important to pause every once in a while, focus on the present, and appreciate where you are in life. If not, a villainous boogeyman might just show up and do it for you.

Reversed: Are you feeling stuck, trapped, or caught up in an unexpected situation that seems dire? Maybe you're facing unforeseen setbacks that have put your progress on hold, or you're feeling listless and lacking direction. Right now, give up a bit of control. Try to work with new circumstances instead of against them, and things will turn out as they're supposed to. You might be happily surprised by where you end up if you go with the flow.

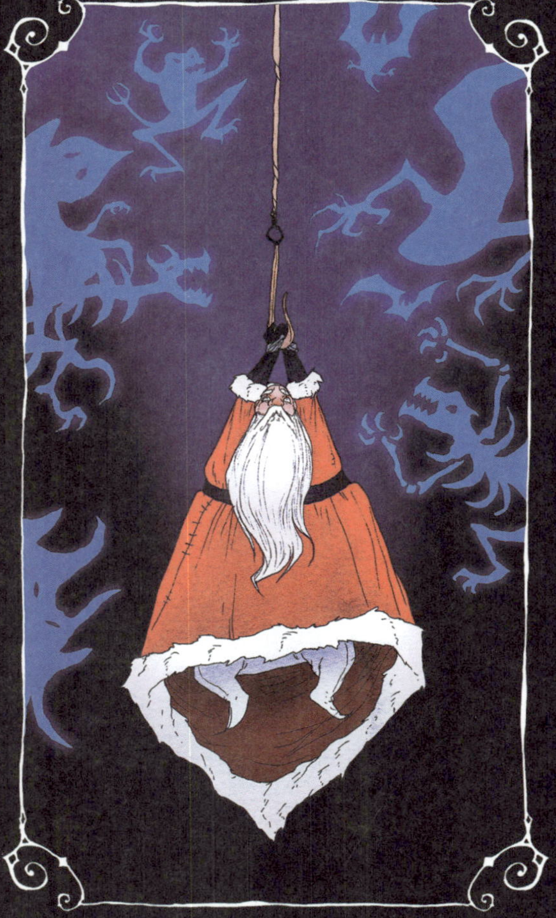

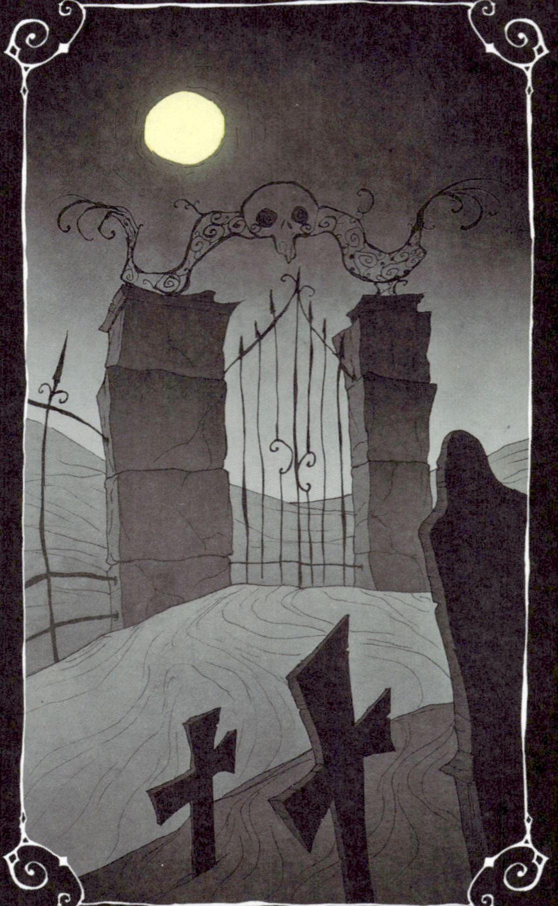

XIII · DEATH

Death is often a feared tarot card, but that's just because it's misunderstood. It's a card of transformation and transition—beginnings and endings. Like the creaky, old gates in Halloween Town's cemetery, the Death tarot card is a spooky symbol of change and transformation.

Upright: You're going through a powerful transition. Whatever sort of big change is happening in your life right now, embrace it, because it will eventually lead to bigger and better things.

Reversed: Are you putting off a life-changing decision? Resisting change is impossible and will only cause harm in the long run. Letting go of the familiar can be tough, but trust that accepting transition will make way for positive, fresh beginnings.

THE MAJOR ARCANA

XIV · TEMPERANCE

Like pouring magical potions into a cauldron, Temperance represents the act of combining different elements together in perfect harmony.

Upright: The message of Temperance is moderation. Now isn't the time for excess or extremes, so make sure you're maintaining balance in your life. Remember, whatever you put out, you'll get back. It's all about give-and-take. Embrace the flow!

Reversed: If life is feeling hectic, it's time to bring things back into balance. Pay attention to areas of your life that may be a little neglected. The recipe for success requires a pinch of self-reflection and a dash of Temperance. Stir thoroughly, and enjoy.

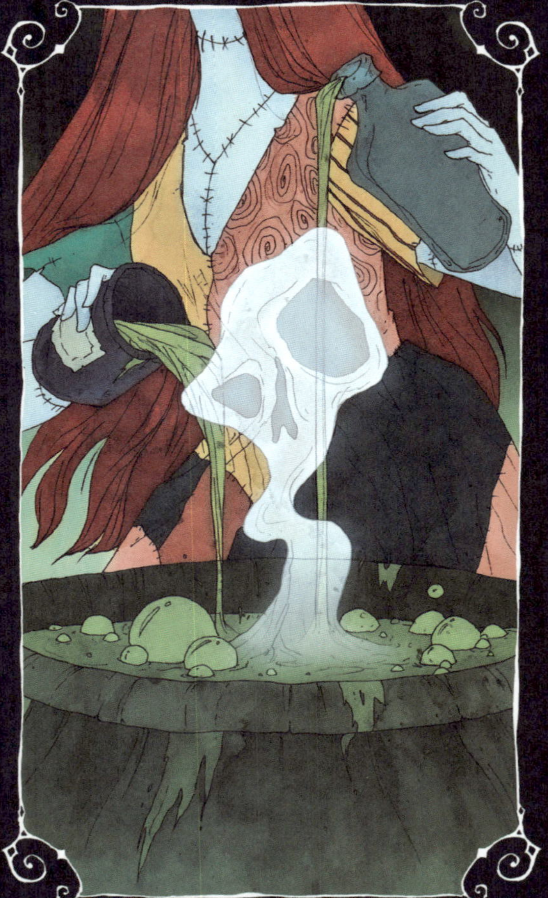

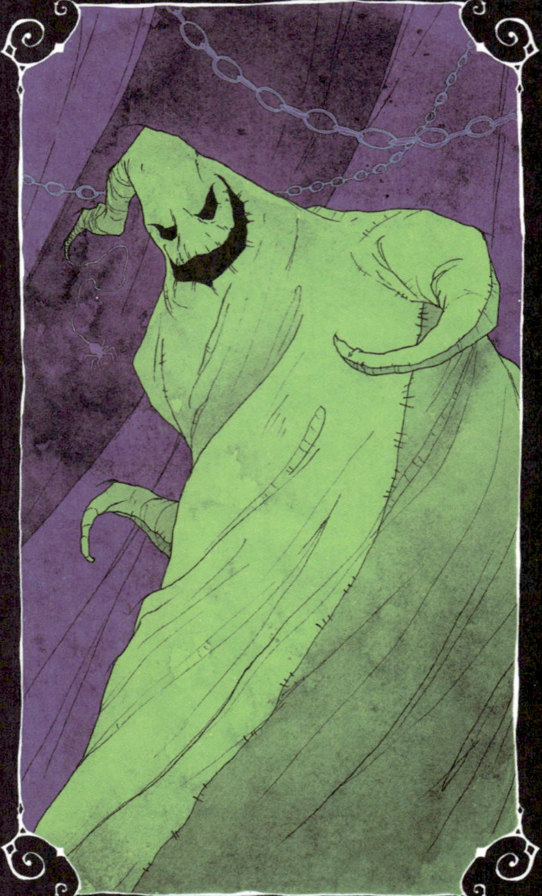

XV · THE DEVIL

The Devil represents temptation, overindulgence, and bad habits, which happen to be some of Oogie Boogie's favorite things!

Upright: If you're caught up in self-indulgence or vice, it's time to rein it in and regain control. Don't gamble with your health and happiness. Remember that instant gratification isn't satisfying in the long term, so come up with a lasting plan for success.

Reversed: Confront what scares you to release yourself from self-sabotaging behaviors that have been holding you back. Keep a level head, and be brave. You may just find the great, big Oogie Boogie in your life isn't as frightening as you think.

THE MAJOR ARCANA

XVI · THE TOWER

Jack plots his Christmas takeover high up in his tower, but his scheme doesn't go according to plan, creating chaos in both the human world and the holiday worlds. The Tower represents unexpected destruction, confusion, and major upheaval that illuminates the truth.

Upright: While you may be feeling blindsided by an unexpected life-changing revelation, trust that this new perspective will ultimately help you. Clarity will come when the dust settles.

Reversed: Sometimes the Tower reversed indicates you're going through a very personal, cataclysmic transformation. Soul-searching and honesty will see you through the fog. Other times, the Tower reversed indicates resistance to the change brought on by catastrophe. Don't fear the unknown! Embrace the inevitable for a smoother transition into brighter days.

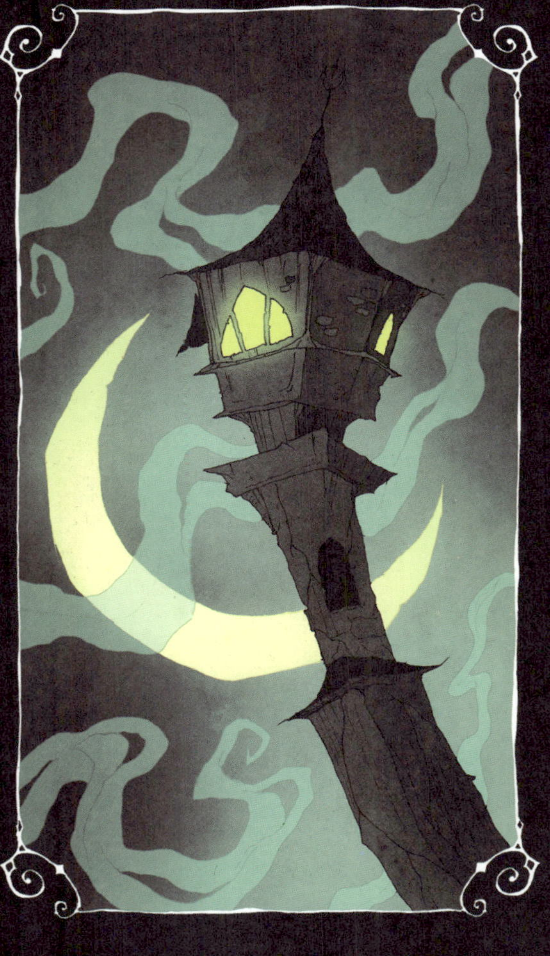

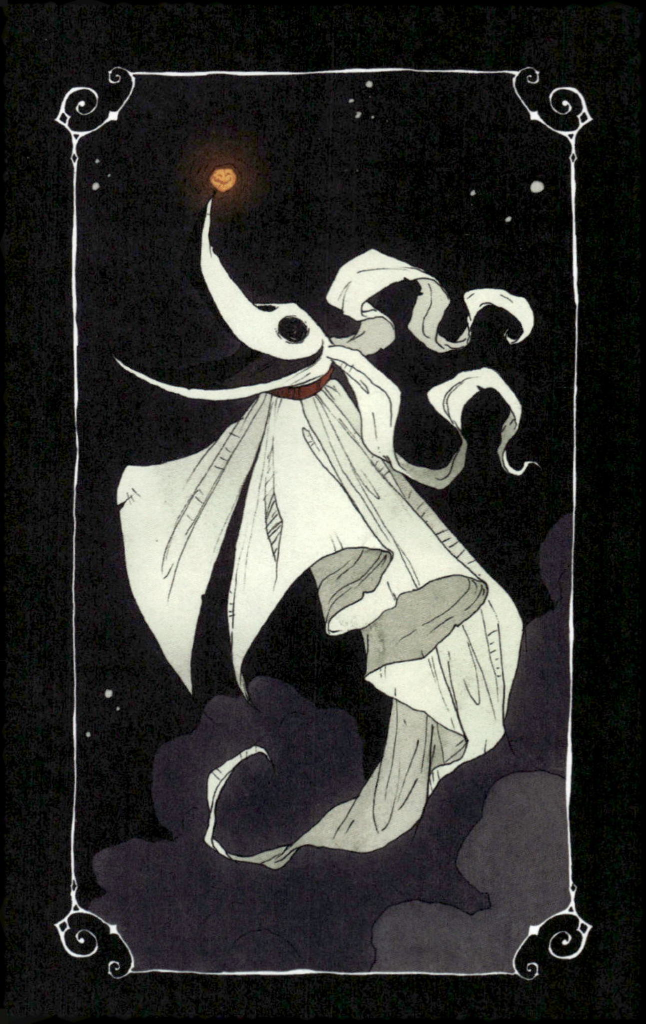

XVII · THE STAR

The Star represents trust, faith, and a newly found clarity. When all feels lost, have hope! Like Zero's glowing jack-o'-lantern nose, the Star will light your way and guide you forward.

Upright: Now is the time to look to the skies and dream. The Star is here to illuminate the visionary in you. Let go of self-doubt that's weighing you down, because inspiration is ready to carry you to new heights.

Reversed: Are you feeling confused, lost, or discouraged? Don't despair! The Star is a comforting beacon of light. Trust in yourself, and you'll find your way out of the fog. Your dreams are still possible—you just need to believe in them again.

THE MAJOR ARCANA

XVIII · THE MOON

Moonlight illuminates Jack in the graveyard as he reflects on his feelings. The Moon represents a great lament, the subconscious, and intuition.

Upright: Analyze complex or confusing situations you find yourself in. Are things really what they seem to be? What's going on under the surface? Beware of deception, and listen to your instincts—they know the truth.

Reversed: In order to move forward, you need to be honest about your feelings, with yourself and others. Expressing yourself will lift a weight off your chest and get you out of a melancholy headspace. The Sun is about to come out, and a new day will bring new possibilities.

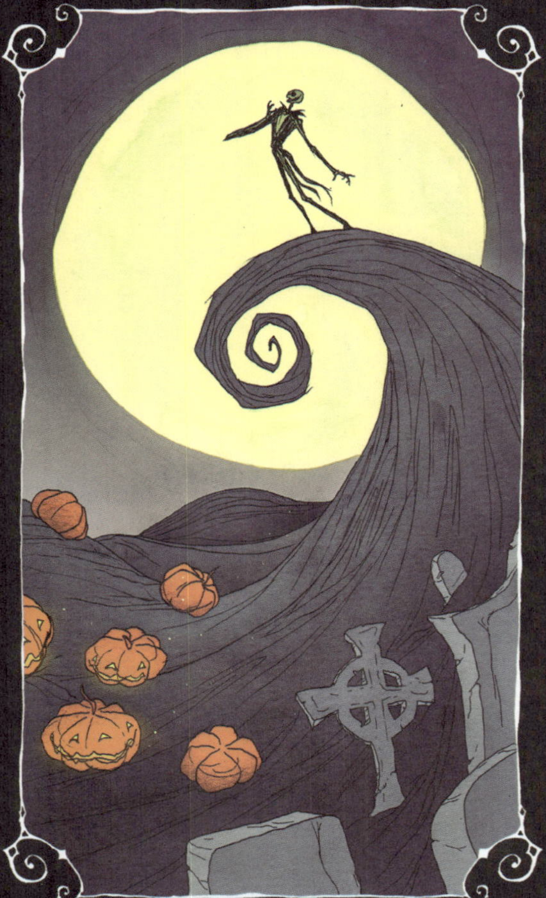

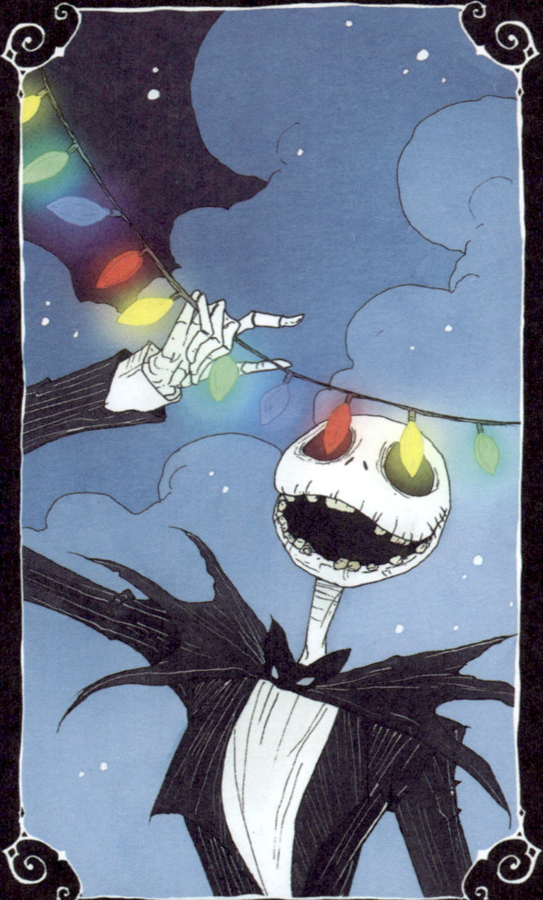

XIX · THE SUN

When cloudy skies pass, the Sun comes out, shining warmth and happiness on everyone's lives. The excitement, renewed energy, and joy Jack experiences when he discovers Christmas Town perfectly embody the energy of the Sun tarot card.

Upright: If you've been sad or troubled lately, the Sun is a sign you're about to feel a very positive shift in your life. Use this rejuvenating energy to reconnect with good friends and enjoy yourself. There's so much enthusiasm in this tarot card. It signifies a powerful time for inspired brainstorming.

Reversed: Reversed, the Sun can either represent reckless idealism and a runaway ego or a lack of joy in your life. Have you become bogged down in day-to-day details? Do something fun and unexpected to shake yourself out of a humdrum mindset.

THE MAJOR ARCANA

XX · JUDGMENT

We all have pivotal decisions to make in our lives. Will yours land you on the naughty list or the nice list?

Upright: Now isn't the time to be hasty and impulsive. Consider your actions and choices carefully, and take time to think things through. Remember that all actions have reactions. Be sensible, and stay true to your conscience.

Reversed: Have you been a little too self-critical lately? Thoughtful reflection can be positive and constructive, but be careful not to take that energy too far and get down on yourself. We all make mistakes! Learn from them, and forgive yourself. You're doing your best.

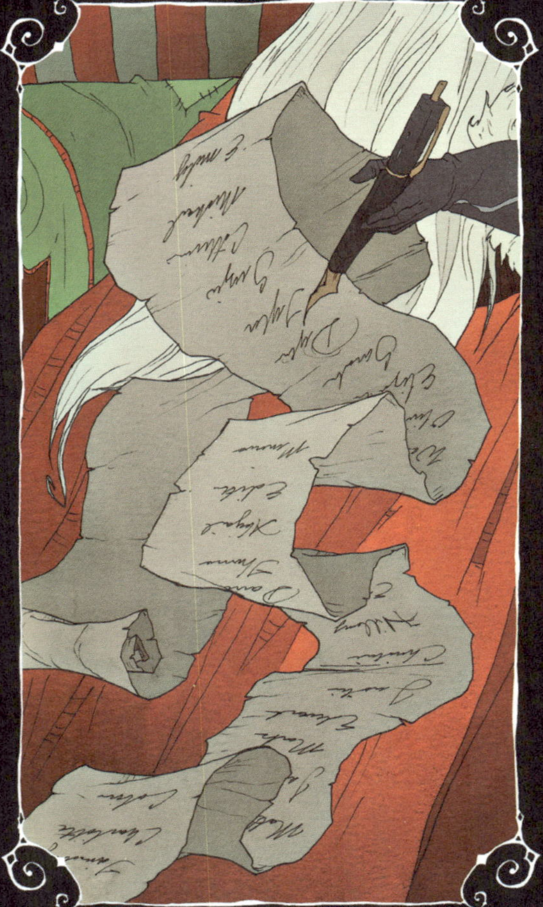

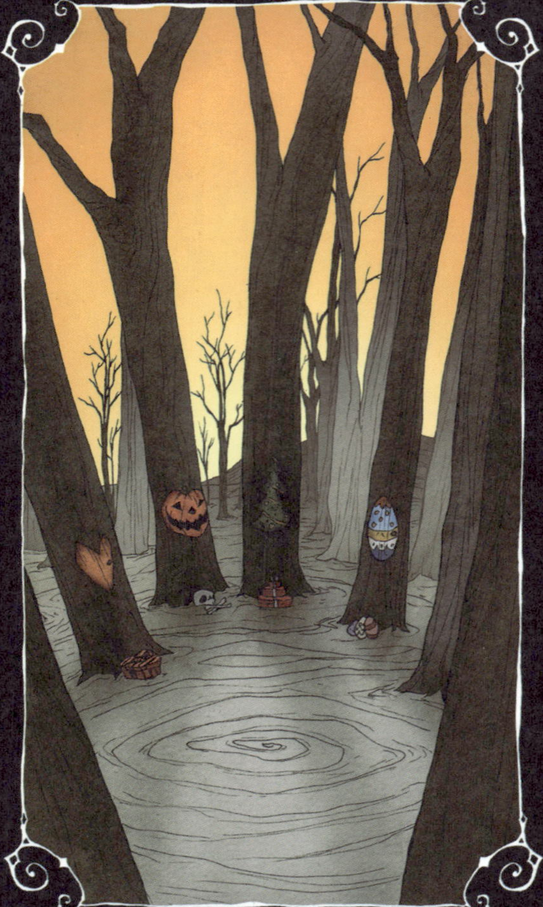

XXI · THE WORLD

The World represents the completion of a long, life-changing adventure. Whether this journey has taken you to magical new places, or you've been on a more personal, internal adventure to self-discovery, you've come out on top. Congratulations!

Upright: You've done it! You've come so far, been through so much, and learned so many powerful lessons along the way. You're feeling satisfied, happy, and whole. Consider sharing your experiences with others. You have the ability to inspire people.

Reversed: If you're finding it difficult to let go of something that was once important to you, remember that endings can be healthy. Sometimes, you need to close one door before you can open another. Who knows? The next step may lead to an adventure more wonderful than you ever imagined.

THE MAJOR ARCANA

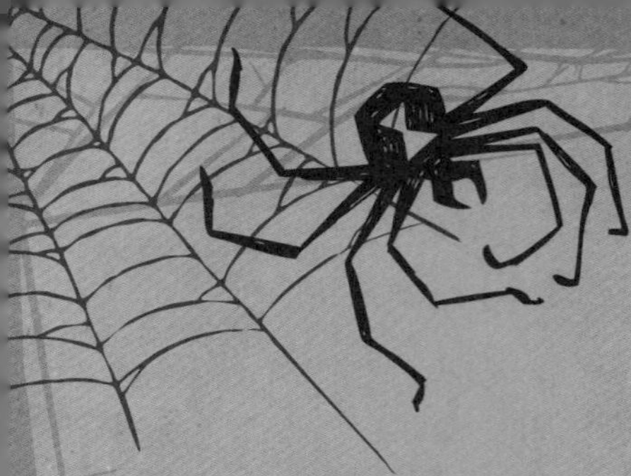

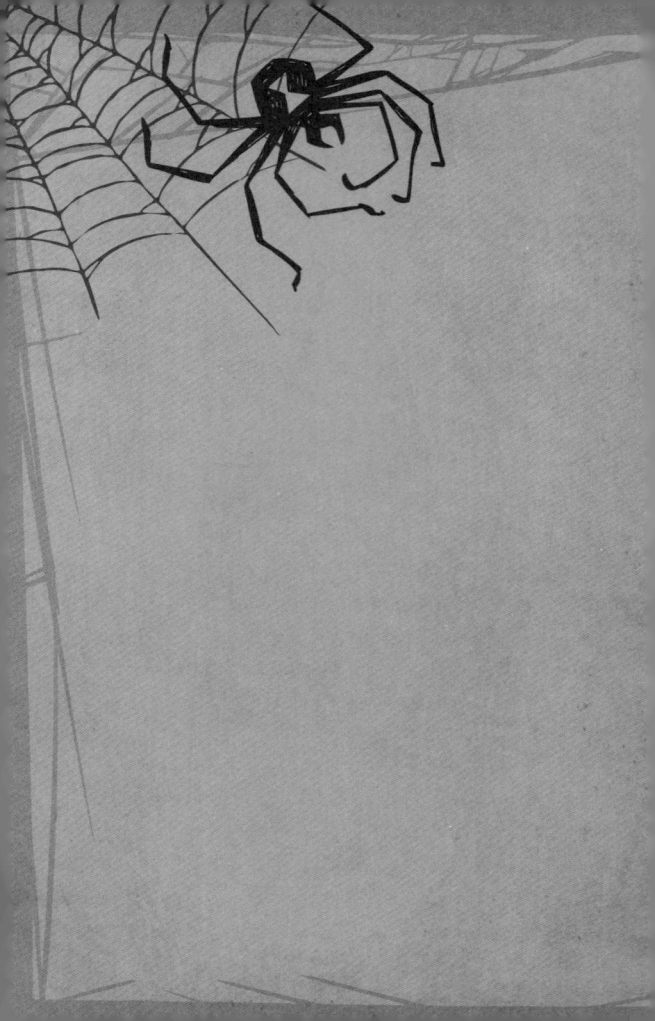

THE MINOR ARCANA

SUIT OF CANDLES

KING OF CANDLES

Upright: The King of Candles is a capable, celebrated leader who focuses on the big picture. Like the Pumpkin King himself, he's a visionary with a knack for bringing people together and inspiring them to work toward a common goal.

Reversed: Here, the King of Candles tunes out the opinions of others and becomes a bit ruthless in the pursuit of what he wants. His impulsiveness and unyielding determination can lead to disaster if he refuses to listen to sensible advice.

QUEEN OF CANDLES

Upright: The Queen of Candles represents a clever, confident person with a strong independent streak. Used to being the center of attention, she's a popular, inspiring leader who brings out the best in everyone. Bringing optimism into any project will invigorate it with the energy it needs to be successful.

Reversed: The reversed Queen of Candles lacks self-confidence. Have you been giving too much attention to the opinions of others? Don't stifle your ideas and lose your voice. Make time for a bit of soul-searching, and express yourself. Don't worry what others may think. You have so much to offer!

SUIT OF CANDLES

KNIGHT OF CANDLES

Upright: The Knight of Candles is a fierce, bold, impulsive figure who breaks down barriers. Full of wild, primal energy, he's feeling inspired and always up for an adventure.

Reversed: Here, the impulsive enthusiasm of the Knight of Candles leads to frustration and chaos. It's time to rein in your wild side, and focus your energy on the journey at hand. You won't make any progress if you don't pay attention to where you're going.

PAGE OF CANDLES

Upright: The Page of Candles represents someone who's full of fresh, innovative, creative ideas. He's ready to soar but may not yet have the solid, stable foundation necessary to move forward and bring those great ideas to life.

Reversed: Reversed, the Page of Candles is dealing with disappointment and frustration. He put a lot of energy and time into something, but things haven't gone according to plan. Don't clip your own wings and give up on your dreams. Instead, strategize and try a new approach.

SUIT OF CANDLES

ACE OF CANDLES

Upright: The Ace of Candles is full of inspired, creative energy. Your ideas are on fire! Now is the perfect time to start a new project. Big opportunities are coming your way. Embrace them with positivity and enthusiasm. Who knows how far they could take you?

Reversed: If you're feeling frustrated because life seems to have gone off the rails, it might be time to backtrack a little and figure out what went wrong. When you set things straight, it will be easier to regain forward momentum.

II OF CANDLES

Upright: As with all II cards, there's an element of decision here. Travel may be on your horizon. Where will you go? Which direction will you take? Spend time planning your next steps. A little preparation now will allow things to go more smoothly later.

Reversed: If you find yourself feeling caught off guard or unprepared for a situation, don't worry about the potential setbacks. Instead, center yourself and keep your eyes on the prize. If you stay focused, you'll navigate through this more easily than you think.

SUIT OF CANDLES

III OF CANDLES

Upright: Now isn't the time to try to do things all by yourself. The III of Candles indicates success will come through cooperation and collaboration. You have a great opportunity in front of you. Make the most of it by putting a little trust in others and being open to their ideas.

Reversed: III of Candles reversed shows a need for broader thinking. Don't limit yourself or sell yourself short! Your potential is infinite. Think bigger, and make a plan for expansion and growth.

THE MINOR ARCANA

IV OF CANDLES

Upright: IV of Candles represents celebration. People are recognizing your accomplishments! You're feeling stable, secure, and comfortable. Be proud of yourself and enjoy the attention, but remember there is still work to be done when the party's over.

Reversed: There's a homey, familiar element to the IV of Candles. Reversed, it can indicate something's gone awry at home. Are you in conflict with a family member? Is your sense of security wavering? Get to the root of the problem, and work to rebuild things from the ground up. A solid foundation creates stability.

SUIT OF CANDLES

V OF CANDLES

Upright: If you find yourself in a collaboration or partnership that's starting to become chaotic or difficult, take a step back. Pointing fingers, shifting blame, and bickering won't move things along. Control your anger, and communicate clearly and rationally to get everyone on the same page.

Reversed: While the upright V of Candles tells of conflict with others, that friction becomes internalized when the card is reversed. Are you feeling at war with yourself? Are you struggling with a tough personal decision? Don't be so hard on yourself, and trust that things will work out in time.

VI OF CANDLES

Upright: Success! This is a victorious card showing all your hard work is paying off, and you're getting the rewards you deserve. Keep the momentum going by turning this self-confidence boost into motivation for your next project.

Reversed: You've been measuring yourself against other people's barometers of success and feeling disappointed. It's time to check in with yourself. What makes you happy? What do you find fulfilling? Reject the status quo, and celebrate your accomplishments without comparing them with anyone else's.

SUIT OF CANDLES

VII OF CANDLES

Upright: VII of Candles shows you might soon be entering into competition. If someone is trying to get between you and your goals, hold your ground. This isn't the time to acquiesce or let your guard down. Know what you want, and work hard to get it.

Reversed: Has your self-confidence taken a hit recently? Are you feeling overwhelmed or exasperated? Don't get so bogged down in the details that you lose sight of the larger picture. Remember how far you've come—you're more than capable of making your dreams come true!

VIII OF CANDLES

Upright: VIII of Candles shows things are changing quickly now. You're feeling industrious and inventive, and heading into a fast-paced time in your life. Use this fresh, inspired energy to transform the mundane into something delightful!

Reversed: VIII of Candles reversed shows it's time to embrace change. Transformation is a good thing, and it's inevitable! Fighting progress won't get you anywhere, so move forward with an open mind. Who knows? Accepting new ways may just lead you to discovering the perfect outlet for your genius.

IX OF CANDLES

Upright: IX of Candles tells of a current need for protection and conservation. If you're going through a challenging time, self-preservation is the name of the game. Guard your energy and resources. But remember you're not alone, and don't be afraid to ask for help.

Reversed: Reversed, IX of Candles shows you're feeling overwhelmed by challenges. Life feels difficult, and nothing seems to be coming as easily as it should. Take comfort in knowing these are short-term problems. Keep going! You'll get through this soon.

X OF CANDLES

Upright: Sometimes, big responsibilities come with big accomplishments. You're succeeding, and that's great! However, this means it's time to work even harder. If you're feeling burdened or overwhelmed, embrace a leadership role, and assign some of the workload to others. You don't have to do it all yourself.

Reversed: You're feeling weighed down by a heavy burden. You perceive it as something you have to deal with alone, but people are standing by, waiting to support you. Let them. You'll feel so much better.

SUIT OF CANDLES

SUIT OF PRESENTS

KING OF PRESENTS

Upright: The King of Presents is the ultimate provider. Through hard work and smart delegation, he meets his goals, and he loves sharing the wealth with others. This card is a call to spread cheer!

Reversed: Reversed, the King of Presents represents someone who doesn't have a healthy relationship with wealth. He's obsessed with accumulating it at any cost and lets his ego get tied up in what he owns. It may be time to step back and reconnect with who you are. All the presents in the world aren't worth compromising your authenticity.

QUEEN OF PRESENTS

Upright: Joyful and content with life, the Queen of Presents is a kind caretaker who has everything she needs. She's stable, prosperous, and living a life of abundance. The Queen of Presents advises you to stay humble, benevolent, and kind.

Reversed: Reversed, the Queen of Presents has difficulty finding the balance between work and home. She feels pulled between the two and unable to give either her full focus. Reevaluate what's really important to you, and adjust your schedule accordingly to avoid frustration and burnout.

SUIT OF PRESENTS

KNIGHT OF PRESENTS

Upright: The Knight of Presents is a hardworking, steadfast person focused on being as productive as he can possibly be. He finds success in his endeavors by sticking to a solid routine. This card advises you to work diligently, and focus on the details.

Reversed: Listless, lost, and lacking motivation, the Knight of Presents reversed represents someone who's lost sight of their goals and needs to rediscover their spark. If you've been isolating yourself lately, it's time to collaborate with others. Accountability and teamwork will help you find your groove again.

PAGE OF PRESENTS

Upright: Have you ever been struck with a great idea when you least expected it? Woken up with a brilliant new scheme or plan for success? The Page of Presents represents someone who's feeling a sudden burst of creative and potentially lucrative inspiration. It's time to bring your brilliant, new vision to life. Stay excited for this journey, but be cautious. You never know what surprises might be waiting for you.

Reversed: Reversed, the Page of Presents is disappointed and frustrated. Things haven't turned out quite as they were expected to. Learn from this experience, cut your losses, and move on. There are more opportunities for success on the horizon!

SUIT OF PRESENTS

ACE OF PRESENTS

Upright: The Ace of Presents shows great things are coming your way! This could refer to a lucrative new job, a gift, or an unexpected monetary windfall. Take full advantage of new opportunities that appear, because the time is right for success.

Reversed: If you're presented with an opportunity that sounds too good to be true, take time to examine it carefully. Things may not be as great as they initially seem. Be discerning, and remember it's okay to decline any offer that doesn't feel like the right fit for you.

THE MINOR ARCANA

II OF PRESENTS

Upright: II of Presents reminds you it's important to prioritize your time. There are only so many hours in a day. Make sure you're giving enough attention to the people and things that mean the most.

Reversed: You're struggling to manage your time, money, or energy, and it's starting to affect you negatively. If you have too much on your plate, reevaluate your commitments. Analyze your expenses and cash flow, delegate tasks, and make meaningful changes that will create balance in your life.

SUIT OF PRESENTS

III OF PRESENTS

Upright: Whether you're making presents for Sandy Claws to hand out on Christmas Eve or working on something a little more mundane, III of Presents indicates it's time to work with others to accomplish your objective.

Reversed: Reversed, III of Presents represents an imbalance within a professional or financial collaboration. If you're working with others on a project, make sure everyone's doing their part. Disaster strikes when things become inequitable. Prioritizing teamwork will get you where you want to go.

IV OF PRESENTS

Upright: IV of Presents represents happiness and stability at home, at work, and within your budget. You're on track and setting yourself up for success by building your plans on solid ground. Say thanks with thoughtful gifts to those who've helped you get here!

Reversed: Is your relationship with money healthy? Is it getting you where you want to go? If not, it may be time to look over your budget and reevaluate your priorities. Make sure you're not spending frivolously if your cash flow can't support it right now.

SUIT OF PRESENTS

V OF PRESENTS

Upright: V of Presents represents material scarcity. If you're in need of a helping hand at work or financially, ask for it. Sometimes, this tarot card shows you're standing in the way of your own success. You'll have more luck if you focus on the positives and keep your head up.

Reversed: You've been going through a tough time financially or professionally, but your luck is finally turning around. Hooray! Lucrative new opportunities come unexpectedly, and just in the nick of time.

VI OF PRESENTS

Upright: 'Tis the season of gift giving! Share your treasures with others, and let your loved ones know how much you appreciate them. It's time to give others the credit they deserve for helping you get where you are today. Generosity will bring you even more success.

Reversed: Reversed, the gift-giving theme of the upright VI of Presents needs to be internalized. Self-love is the name of the game. Treat yourself to something you've been wanting. You deserve to enjoy the rewards of your hard work.

SUIT OF PRESENTS

VII OF PRESENTS

Upright: VII of Presents reminds you to keep your long-term goals in mind. You have a long path ahead of you and are working hard to set yourself up for success. Careful planning now will lead to big rewards later.

Reversed: It can be discouraging to work hard without seeing immediate results, but keep at it. The best rewards often take time and a lot of work to manifest. Remember why you started, and keep going. You'll get there!

VIII OF PRESENTS

Upright: VIII of Presents represents the act of working hard to learn new skills. Like a Christmas elf building toys for Sandy Claws, you'll perfect your craft through careful repetition and attention to detail. Tasks will get easier for you the more often you practice. Keep going!

Reversed: Attention to detail is great until it turns into shrewd perfectionism. Step back, and try not to focus so much on the minutiae. Make sure the big picture is on track before getting lost in the details.

SUIT OF PRESENTS

IX OF PRESENTS

Upright: IX of Presents represents material abundance. You've made your dreams come true and are reaping the rewards of your hard work. Now that you have everything you need, it's important to set yourself up for sustained success by managing your income wisely.

Reversed: This card reversed reminds you of your value. Don't sell yourself short! Make sure you're getting the compensation you deserve. Believe in your skills and abilities. What you have to offer is important. Adjust accordingly.

THE MINOR ARCANA

X OF PRESENTS

Upright: X of Presents is a card of completion and wealth. It represents a happy home life, lasting success, and financial abundance. Take the X of Presents as a sign things are going to work out in your favor.

Reversed: Reversed, this card indicates you may have an unhealthy relationship with wealth. Are you acting like the Giant Snake, encircling your vast treasure and unwilling to share? Remember you didn't get here by yourself. You had help and support along the way, and now it's your turn to help and support others.

SUIT OF PRESENTS

SUIT OF NEEDLES

KING OF NEEDLES

Upright: The King of Needles has brains, logic, and determination. He's deeply respected but sometimes feared for his cold, shrewd tendencies. When this card comes forward, take it as a sign to let reason and sensibility guide you, instead of letting your emotions get the best of you.

Reversed: Reversed, the King of Needles is cold, calculating, and egotistical. He lets his convictions and visions go to his head and has a major superiority complex. Make sure you're acting in accordance with your conscience and treating others with the respect they deserve.

QUEEN OF NEEDLES

Upright: The Queen of Needles is intelligent, intellectual, and sensible. She takes time to make up her own mind and isn't easily swayed by trends, fads, or popular opinion. Fair and practical, the Queen of Needles shouldn't be underestimated. This card is a call to remember how strong you really are.

Reversed: Reversed, the Queen of Needles becomes sharp and cruel. She can be callous and coldhearted and uses her considerable brainpower to manipulate others. Prone to volatility and emotional outbursts, she needs to regain composure and keep a level head to avoid major conflict.

SUIT OF NEEDLES

KNIGHT OF NEEDLES

Upright: The Knight of Needles has a smooth, devil-may-care, cavalier attitude. He's clever and quick-witted, and has the maturity and focus to back up his brilliant ideas with decisive action. Put your energy into maintaining the pace of your forward momentum, and stop at nothing to see things through.

Reversed: Reversed, the Knight of Needles is unfocused and lacks follow-through. Scatterbrained, he is overwhelmed by the unfinished tasks he leaves in his wake. Instead of spending energy starting new projects impulsively, complete what's already begun.

THE MINOR ARCANA

PAGE OF NEEDLES

Upright: The Page of Needles represents a cunning, curious personality archetype. Like Lock, Shock, and Barrel, the Page of Needles has wit and cleverness but lacks the maturity to realize his way isn't always the best way.

Reversed: Reversed, the Page of Needles becomes a know-it-all whose ego gets in the way of success. He doesn't keep his promises and often passes the blame for his own mistakes to others. Snide and manipulative, the reversed Page of Needles is childish, cold, and self-interested. Remember, cooperation and humility will get you further than bulldozing others.

SUIT OF NEEDLES

ACE OF NEEDLES

Upright: The Ace of Needles represents a major eureka moment. If you're feeling innovative and inspired, run with it! This is a time of mental breakthroughs and revolutionary, clear insight. Make sure to jot down all your brilliant ideas.

Reversed: Have you been feeling lost in a fog? Dazed? Aimless? Confused? Consider what you really want, and come up with a realistic plan to get it. Giving yourself a goal will help you find the motivation and focus you're lacking.

II OF NEEDLES

Upright: Something heavy is on your mind. You've been racking your brain over a predicament, trying to come up with a solution that benefits everyone involved. Make sure you're seeing things as they really are. You need all the facts before you can make up your mind.

Reversed: You're not seeing eye to eye with someone in your life, and things are coming to a head. You've communicated your thoughts and feelings, and so have they, but you're still in disagreement. Sometimes, all you can do is give your best advice and be supportive, without standing in the way. Ultimately, you can't control what other people decide to do.

SUIT OF NEEDLES

III OF NEEDLES

Upright: This is a card of heartbreak, betrayal, and wounded feelings. If a situation is making you feel like needles are piercing your heart, take care of yourself. Express yourself, and work through your feelings in healthy ways. This hurts now, but it won't forever.

Reversed: III of Needles reversed symbolizes coming to terms with the past. It's time to pluck the needles out of your heart, and let it heal. Nurse your wounds, and go forward.

IV OF NEEDLES

Upright: The main message of this card is: rest. Whether you're recovering from a recent battle or need to recharge and prepare for the future, it's time to pause and collect yourself.

Reversed: Here, the restful energy of the IV of Needles card becomes static. Are you feeling stuck? Have you reached a plateau? It's important to shake yourself out of your routine. When you take a different perspective, you'll see you have all kinds of opportunities around you.

SUIT OF NEEDLES

V OF NEEDLES

Upright: This is the ultimate battle card. Are you fighting an Oogie Boogie in your life? Conflict can be uncomfortable, but sometimes, it's inevitable. You'll need to be agile and clever to gain the upper hand. Good luck!

Reversed: V of Needles reversed represents the period after a battle when it's time to shake hands and move on. You've had a moment to settle your bets and cool off. Let bygones be bygones, and move on with your head held high.

VI OF NEEDLES

Upright: VI of Needles usually indicates you've been through a difficult time. Have you recently been in conflict with someone or experienced an unexpected setback? It's time to pick up the pieces and get on track again.

Reversed: You're avoiding taking action on something, which is making you uneasy. This card reversed often represents resistance or a delay that won't benefit you in the long run. Leaving what's comfortable and familiar can be scary. Trust that this change will be worth the temporary discomfort.

SUIT OF NEEDLES

VII OF NEEDLES

Upright: VII of Needles often represents sneaky behavior. You may need to play your cards close to your chest. If you're trying to solve a problem, think outside the box. Sometimes, the obvious, conventional path isn't the one that will take you where you want to go.

Reversed: VII of Needles shows up reversed when it's time to face the truth. You know it's better to be honest with yourself in the long run. Acknowledging the reality and working through it will benefit you in the end. Be brave.

VIII OF NEEDLES

Upright: VIII of Needles represents the feeling of restriction. Have hope—all's not lost. Even if you're feeling trapped or stifled, and life seems to be unraveling at the seams, remember that you have the power to free yourself of what's holding you back and stitch yourself back together.

Reversed: Reversed, the card indicates self-deprecation. You're being too hard on yourself! You're full of potential, and opportunities are all around you. Believe in yourself, and don't be afraid to go out on a limb to reach what you want.

IX OF NEEDLES

Upright: Nightmares, worries, fear—IX of Needles shows up when you're feeling dread. Muster your courage and face your fears. You might just find the Clown with the Tear-Away Face is not as scary in the light of day.

Reversed: Has your confidence been dealt a blow recently? If you're feeling low, you may be your own biggest bully. Start focusing on your positive qualities instead of fixating on perceived negative ones. A shift in perspective is what's needed to get you out of despair.

X OF NEEDLES

Upright: X of Needles indicates something is coming to a painful ending. Whether this refers to a friendship, relationship, project, or job, you may be left with heavy emotions. Give yourself time to grieve, but trust that it's for the best. Fresh beginnings are ahead!

Reversed: When reversed, the painful ending indicated by the upright X of Needles is stalled. Don't put off the inevitable—dragging it out will only make this harder. Make a clean break, and move on to new, better things.

SUIT OF POTIONS

KING OF POTIONS

Upright: The King of Potions is a loyal, sensible problem solver. Embody the energy of the King of Potions by maintaining a healthy balance between the head and heart. Be logical, but stay compassionate and kind.

Reversed: The reversed King of Potions is emotionally turbulent, and his intense, unpredictable moods can harm those around him. If you're feeling overwhelmed, try working through your feelings in healthy ways. Take care to anticipate your responses to make sure your feelings don't get the better of you.

QUEEN OF POTIONS

Upright: The Queen of Potions is a calm, cool, and caring gal who's motivated by compassion. She moves with grace and control through troubled waters. Sometimes, this card can be a sign to listen to your intuition. You're more perceptive and capable than you think.

Reversed: Reversed, the Queen of Potions becomes volatile, exasperated, and overly emotional. This card could be a sign that a major relationship in your life is out of balance. Clear communication will help you sort things out. Remember: You're strong and capable!

SUIT OF POTIONS

KNIGHT OF POTIONS

Upright: The Knight of Potions is a graceful, effortlessly fluid figure who backs up his dreams with focused momentum and action. A revolutionary with a kind heart, the Knight of Potions is here to encourage you to find your passion. It's time to explore ideas and causes that move you.

Reversed: Reversed, the Knight of Potions becomes sulky, gloomy, and brooding. This is often caused by a big disappointment. Take time to really think about your options before acting on them. Relationships can get sticky when decisions are made emotionally rather than logically.

THE MINOR ARCANA

PAGE OF POTIONS

Upright: The Page of Potions goes through life (and death?) with childlike curiosity and hopeful enthusiasm. Unleash your creativity, and charge forward in pursuit of the things you're passionate about. Sometimes, this card represents the beginning of a new relationship or close friendship.

Reversed: The Page of Potions reversed doesn't always handle his emotions well. He can be childish, naive, and even a little selfish. This card appears reversed when you're in need of a new emotional outlet. Now is a great time to explore creative new ways of expressing yourself.

SUIT OF POTIONS

ACE OF POTIONS

Upright: You're feeling inspired, creative, and intuitive. Someone special may be entering the picture soon. Whether this person ends up being a love interest or a great new friend, things are happening just as they should now. Stay curious, pay attention, and enjoy the moment.

Reversed: You're experiencing some sort of emotional imbalance. If you've been repressing your feelings and ideas, know that now isn't the time to bottle things up. Sharing your thoughts will lead to relief and positive connections. On the other hand, if you've been letting your feelings run away with you, it's time to rein them in, center yourself, and regain control.

II OF POTIONS

Upright: You're in complete harmony with someone special in your life. Whether this is a work-related partnership, a romantic relationship, or a friendship, it's a positive for you both. Be sure to stay supportive of each other! This connection has major growth potential.

Reversed: Have things been feeling a little off between you and someone important in your life? Examine your own needs and motivations. How do you really feel about this relationship? Are you being honest, compassionate, and supportive? Are they? Give yourself time to reflect, take a deep breath, and try talking things out. If equilibrium can't be reached, moving on alone may be the best course of action.

III OF POTIONS

Upright: Now is a great time to get together with supportive, fun people, and enjoy yourself. Live it up a little! Any collaborations you find yourself in are supercharged now, so get ready for unexpected breakthroughs. Host a brainstorming session, and let creative energy and inspiration flow freely.

Reversed: Are you feeling like you're on the outside looking in? If there's a disconnect between you and a group of people, don't force things. Some connections just aren't meant to last, and that's okay. Happiness comes from staying true to yourself, even if it means going it alone for a little while. Your crew is out there!

IV OF POTIONS

Upright: IV of Potions indicates there's a decision to be made, but remember, you don't have to accept everything you're offered. Listen to your intuition, and don't be afraid to decline opportunities that don't feel right. Make sure you know what you're signing up for by carefully reading the fine print, especially when faced with offers that seem too good to be true.

Reversed: Introspection can be really positive, but make sure to stay connected to the world around you. Take a moment alone, check in with yourself, and gather your thoughts, then move back into being social. Isolation will do more harm than good.

V OF POTIONS

Upright: Disappointments and setbacks have you feeling depressed. Something hasn't gone according to plan. Rather than feeling glum and remorseful about what can't be changed, accept the circumstances and look for a way forward. There are new opportunities waiting for you.

Reversed: Reversed, this card indicates personal mistakes have been made. It's time to recognize these missteps and forgive yourself. You did the best you could with the knowledge you had at the time. Instead of wallowing in regret, do what you can to right your wrongs, and take care not to make the same mistakes again. You're wiser because of this experience.

VI OF POTIONS

Upright: Close your eyes, and think of a time in your past when you were truly, incandescently happy—downright joyful, even. It's time to recreate that feeling! Reconnect with the little things that make life fun and leave you bubbling over with simple, pure happiness. Sometimes, VI of Potions can be a sign you'll soon be reuniting with someone important from your past. Enjoy the memories!

Reversed: Nostalgia is in the air—and it could be clouding your thinking. While reminiscing about the past can help you appreciate the present, keep in mind it's easy to romanticize past connections and events. Take care to keep your wistful thinking based in reality.

SUIT OF POTIONS

VII OF POTIONS

Upright: Dreaming can be a powerful act of manifestation. Let your mind wander a little. What adventures do you want to go on? Where do you want them to take you? Visualize your best life, and then put real action behind making those visions a reality.

Reversed: You have a lot of options in front of you, and each of them seems dreamier than the last. It's easy to get caught up in idealistic thinking now, so make sure you're seeing things as they really are. Don't be fooled by smoke and mirrors. If you find yourself presented with something that seems too good to be true, be careful, because it probably is.

VIII OF POTIONS

Upright: VIII of Potions comes forward when a dream, once achieved, isn't quite as fulfilling as expected. You worked so hard for this, but you're still not satisfied. Take some time to reflect on your current feelings and needs, because they may have changed. Adjust your situation accordingly.

Reversed: Reversed, VIII of Potions indicates you have a choice to make. Something in your life has reached a tipping point. Will you tough it out, or is it time to move on? Only you know the answer, but sometimes, it's best to let sleeping dogs lie, bury the past, and move on.

SUIT OF POTIONS

IX OF POTIONS

Upright: Congrats! Your wishes are being granted. Your lucky stars have aligned, and things are finally falling into place. It's time to enjoy yourself and appreciate the magic in your life. If only you could bottle this feeling!

Reversed: IX of Potions reversed is a call to check your motivations. Don't worry so much about impressing others and gaining their approval. Lasting happiness comes from authenticity and staying true to yourself. The people who are supposed to be in your life will appreciate you just as you are.

X OF POTIONS

Upright: An important relationship, friendship, or family connection is finding its stride. You're both feeling supported, understood, and appreciated. Nurture this connection, and remember to give as much as you take to maintain balance.

Reversed: Is a relationship in your life in hot water? If you feel like you're floundering, pause and think. Has there been a communication breakdown? Have your goals or needs changed? Have theirs? Stop treading water, and dive below the surface to discover what's really at the heart of the problem.

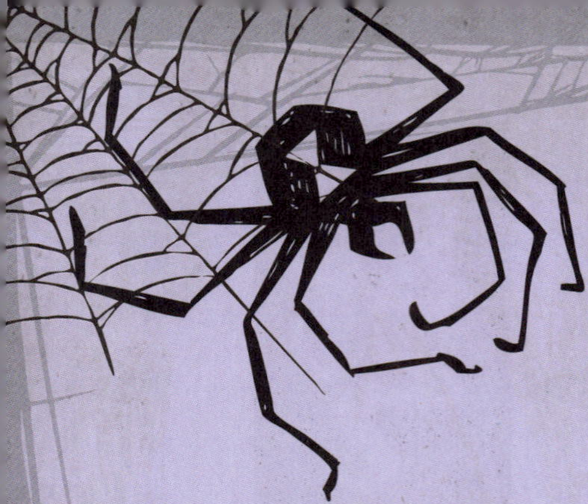

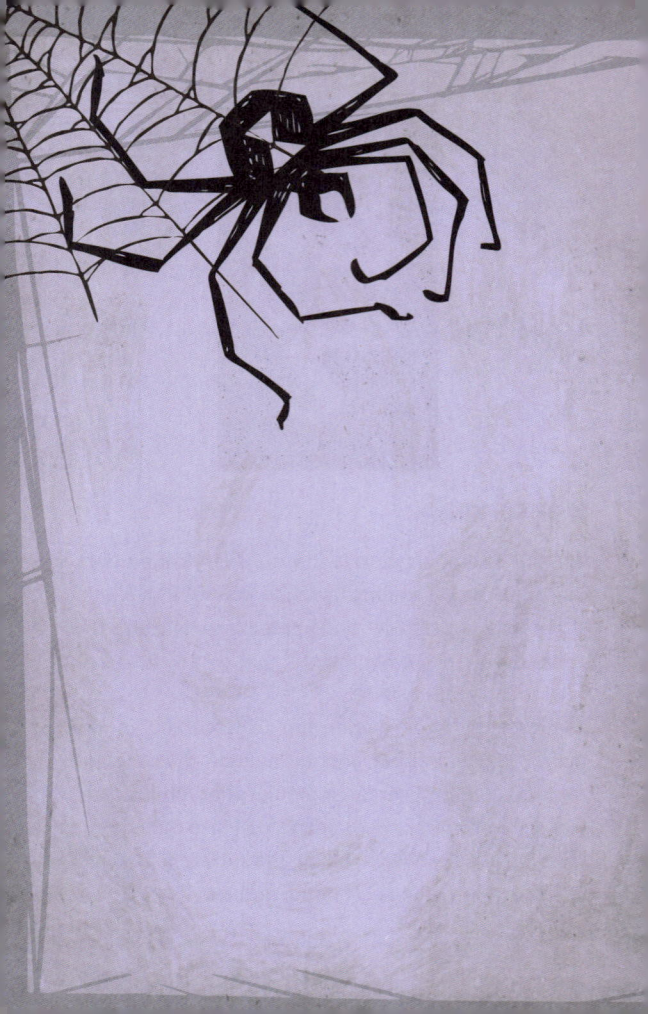

TAROT READINGS

One of the most exciting things about reading tarot—and possibly one of the reasons it's so popular and widespread—is that it can be personalized to suit your style. There are no rules. Use it intuitively, in whatever way feels right to you. Read tarot as often or infrequently as you like. Make it a ritualistic, sacred practice, or take out your deck casually and read the cards with friends. It's all up to you—that's the magic of it.

CARING FOR YOUR DECK

Most tarot readers agree it's important to energetically cleanse your deck regularly, especially if you read tarot for other people. Cleansing your deck leaves you with a clean slate, so your next tarot session will be fresh, clear, and unencumbered by the energy of previous readings.

There are many methods you can use to cleanse your tarot deck. Feel free to experiment with them, and choose the method that resonates with you. Smoke cleansing refers to the act of passing the tarot deck through the smoke of sacred herbs, such as sage, lavender, or palo santo. Placing your deck in moonlight overnight can cleanse and refresh your cards. Many agree the light of a full moon is the most powerful, but any moonlight will do the job. Another option is to use crystals; selenite and black tourmaline make wonderful cleansing tools. Keep them on or around your deck when it's not in use to make sure it's fresh and ready for the next reading.

PREPARING TO READ TAROT

Every good tarot reading begins with a question. You can ask the cards anything and everything: What needs to happen for this relationship to reach its full potential? How should I prepare for my big interview? Is it a good idea to have Lock, Shock, and Barrel kidnap Sandy Claws so I can take over Christmas? Tarot can give you useful insight and advice about any situation, friendship, or relationship you find yourself in.

Begin tarot readings by relaxing and clearing your head. Meditate, take a relaxing bath, or close your eyes for a few moments. Breathe slowly and deeply. When you're ready, ask your question, and shuffle the tarot deck. Some people shuffle the cards like playing cards, while others use an overhand shuffle to avoid bending them. You can even spread them out on a large surface and rifle through them to choose cards intuitively.

When your question has been asked and your cards have been shuffled, it's time to draw cards and lay them out in a tarot spread. Tarot spreads are the specific ways cards are arranged as they're drawn. Here are a few spreads to help you get started.

PREPARING TO READ TAROT

THE SPREADS

EUREKA!

This simple tarot spread will help inspire you when you're feeling stuck in a rut or bored with routine. Whether your *eureka!* moment involves an exciting quest to take over Christmas or something a little less dramatic and harrowing, this tarot spread will stimulate your imagination.

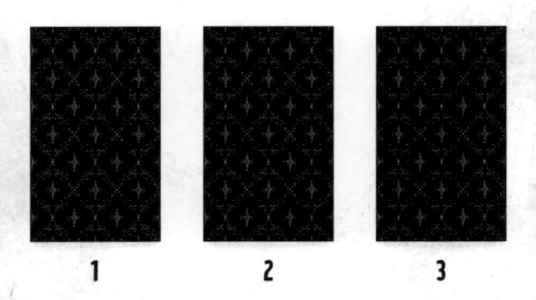

1   **2**   **3**

TAROT READINGS

1. LAMENT

This tarot card represents the aspect of your current situation that needs to change in order for you to feel more creative and energized. It shows why you're feeling a little uninspired.

2. EUREKA

This card represents the nature of your next creative epiphany.

3. SANDY CLAWS

This card gives you a peek into the future by showing you where your big eureka moment will take you.

A PEEK BEHIND THE CYCLOPS'S EYE

A Peek Behind the Cyclops's Eye is a great tarot spread to use when you want to find out what's happening underneath the surface of a situation or relationship. It shows hidden aspects and themes at play to give you a fuller understanding of the true nature of things.

2

3

1

TAROT READINGS

1. THE EYE

This tarot card represents what appears to be going on. It's the base card that shows your current perception of the situation.

2. WHAT'S HIDDEN

This card shows the nature of an important hidden aspect of the situation.

3. ADVICE

This card gives you advice to keep in mind while handling the situation.

BLOWN TO SMITHEREENS

Sometimes, one door has to close before you can enter the next phase of your life. This tarot spread is designed to give you the clarity you need to realize what to hold on to, what to let go, and what to expect from the future. Endings make way for new beginnings and create room for you to become your best self—embrace them!

1. SHOT DOWN

This card reveals what you need to end, move on from, or leave behind.

2. OOGIE'S LOOSE THREAD

This card shows the reason for this ending, and why you need a fresh start.

3. JACK'S ALIVE!

This card represents what you stand to gain from letting go and making room for better things.

4. LESSON LEARNED

This card gives you insight into what you'll learn from this experience.

5. MEANT TO BE

This card reveals the future—what's waiting for you on the other side of this transition.

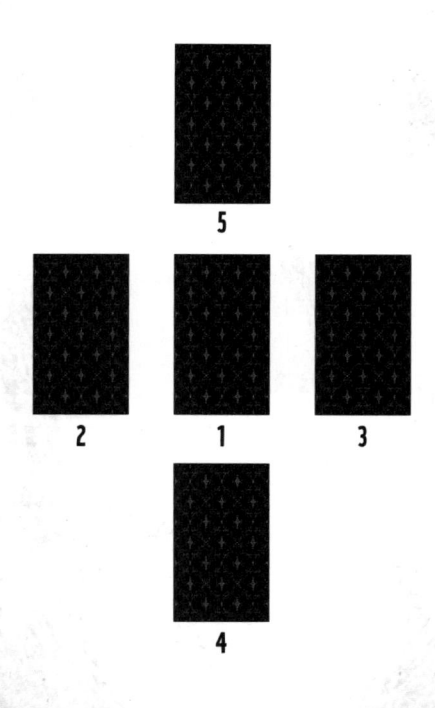

5

2   **1**   **3**

4

THE SPREADS

ABOUT THE AUTHOR

Minerva Siegel is the author of *Tarot for Self-Care: How to Use Tarot to Manifest Your Best Self*. She writes about subjects such as tarot, witchcraft, and living with disabilities for both print magazines and large online publications like Elite Daily. She has been a guest on podcasts such as *The Queer Witch Podcast* and *The Now Age Podcast* with Ruby Warrington. When not writing, she spends her days practicing divination and drinking rose lattes in the Victorian house she shares with her husband and their rescued pack of misfit dogs. You can find her on Instagram using her online handle @SpookyFatBabe.

ABOUT THE ILLUSTRATOR

Hugo Award-winning illustrator **Abigail Larson** specializes in gothic fantasy illustration using a unique mix of traditional and digital media. Her work has been featured in galleries throughout the United States and Europe, and she's worked with Sideshow Collectibles, Syfy, Universal, Titan Comics, Llewellyn Worldwide, DC Comics, and Dark Horse Comics.

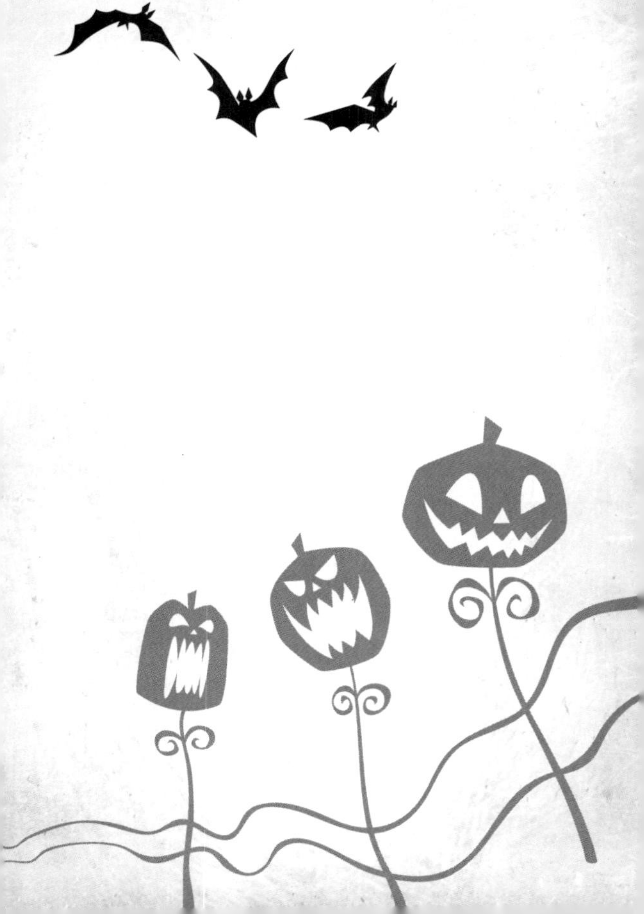

TITAN
BOOKS

144 Southwark Street
London SE1 0UP
www.titanbooks.com

Find us on Facebook: www.facebook.com/TitanBooks
Follow us on Twitter: @TitanBooks

© 2022 Disney

All rights reserved. Published by Titan Books, London, in 2022.

No part of this book may be reproduced in any form without written permission from the publisher.

A CIP catalogue record for this title is available from the British Library.

ISBN: 9781803364117

Insight Editions, in association with Roots of Peace, will plant two trees for each tree used in the manufacturing of this book. Roots of Peace is an internationally renowned humanitarian organization dedicated to eradicating land mines worldwide and converting war-torn lands into productive farms and wildlife habitats. Roots of Peace will plant two million fruit and nut trees in Afghanistan and provide farmers there with the skills and support necessary for sustainable land use.

Manufactured in China by Insight Editions

10 9 8 7 6 5 4 3 2 1